What's the difference?
Reptiles

Stephen Savage

RSVP
RAINTREE
STECK-VAUGHN
P U B L I S H E R S
A Steck-Vaughn Company

Austin, Texas
www.steck-vaughn.com

What's the difference?

Amphibians Insects
Birds Mammals
Fish Reptiles

Cover: An eyelash viper living in the tropical rain forest and (inset) a tortoise

Title Page: A saltwater crocodile and (below) a chameleon

Contents page: A frilled lizard

Published by Raintree Steck-Vaughn Publishers, an imprint of Steck-Vaughn Company

Printed in Italy. Bound in the United States.
1 2 3 4 5 6 7 8 9 0 04 03 02 01 00

Library of Congress Cataloging-in-Publication Data
Savage, Stephen.
Reptiles / Stephen Savage.
    p.   cm.—(What's the difference?)
    Includes bibliographical references and index.
    Summary: Describes the physical characteristics common to reptiles and highlights differences among various species, discussing habitats, methods of getting around, feeding habits, and life cycles.
    ISBN 0-7398-1358-7 (hard)
    0-7398-2037-0 (soft)
    1. Reptiles—Juvenile literature.
    [1. Reptiles.]
    I. Title. II. Series.
    QL644.2.S3   2000
    597.9—dc21   99-044323

Illustrations by: Mark Whitchurch

Contents

What a Difference!

There are four kinds of reptiles. They are lizards and snakes; crocodilians, including crocodiles and alligators; turtles and tortoises; and tuataras. These four kinds of reptiles are very different in shape, size, and color.

Although a tortoise looks very different from a snake, both have similar reptile features.

◄ The giant tortoise feeds on plants and fruit. It can grow more than 4 ft. (1.2 m) long and may weigh more than 550 lbs. (250 kg).

Reptile characteristics

- Reptiles have dry, usually scaly skin. In some cases the skin forms a hard shell.
- Reptiles are cold-blooded. They depend on the sun to heat their bodies.
- They shed their skin as they grow.
- Most have no eyelids.
- Most reptiles lay eggs on land.

⚠ The rattlesnake shakes its tail when alarmed, sounding a rattle that warns attackers to keep away from its poisonous bite.

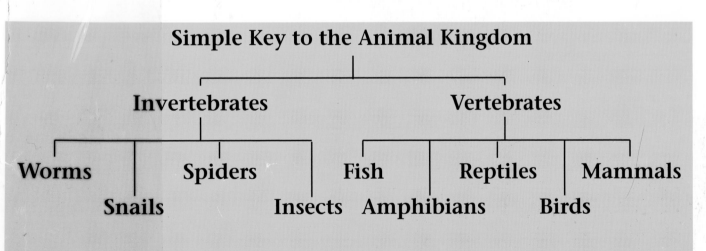

Simple Key to the Animal Kingdom

Invertebrates — Vertebrates

Worms   Spiders   Fish   Reptiles   Mammals

Snails   Insects   Amphibians   Birds

An **Invertebrate** is an animal that does not have a backbone.
A **Vertebrate** is an animal that has a backbone.

Where Reptiles Live

Reptiles live in forests, grasslands, deserts, rivers, and oceans. They live almost everywhere in the world except the Antarctic, which is too cold.

▼ An American alligator in Florida

Living in different habitats

- Alligators have a flattened tail, which helps them to swim. They also have four legs for walking on land.

- The sidewinder snake raises most of its body off the scorching desert sand as it moves, so it doesn't get too hot.

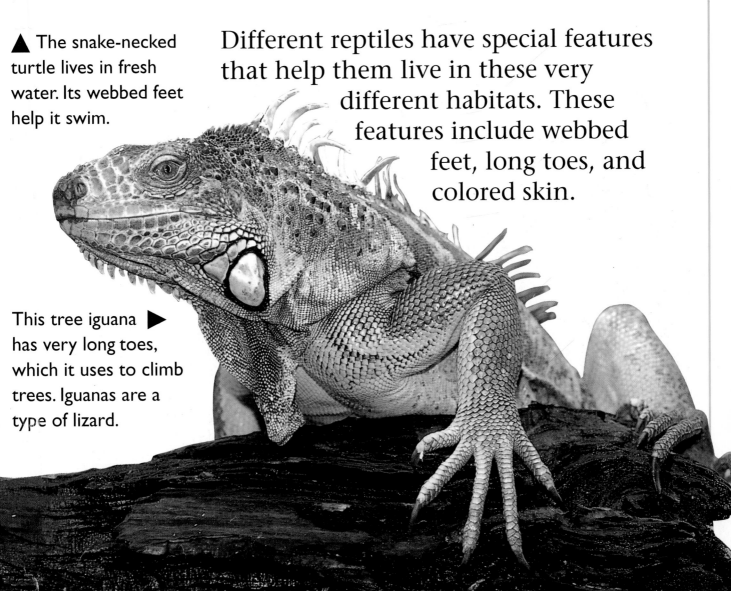

▲ The snake-necked turtle lives in fresh water. Its webbed feet help it swim.

Different reptiles have special features that help them live in these very different habitats. These features include webbed feet, long toes, and colored skin.

This tree iguana ▶ has very long toes, which it uses to climb trees. Iguanas are a type of lizard.

Catching a Meal

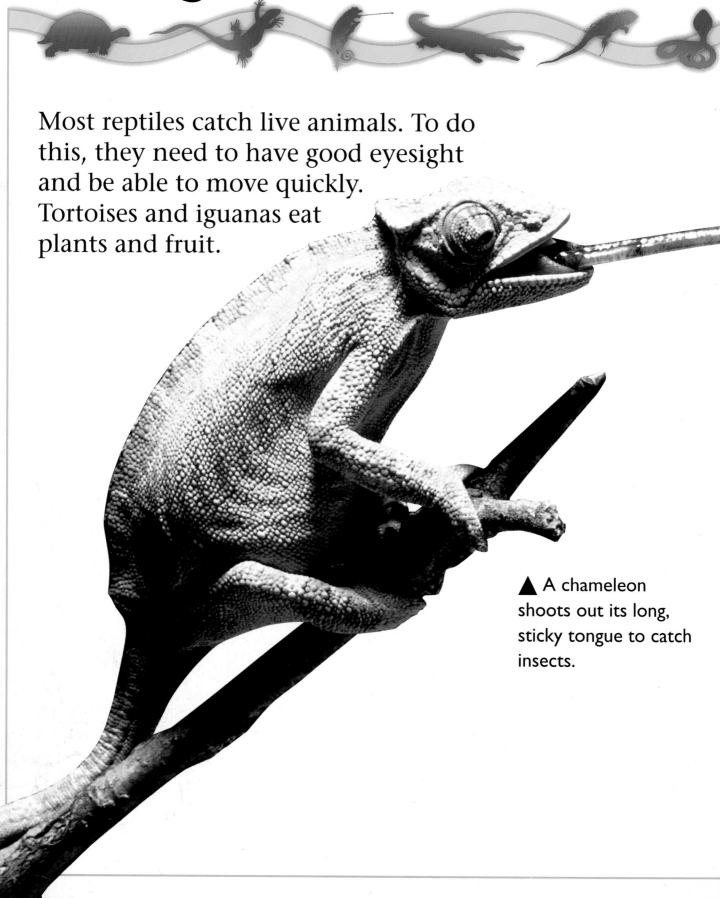

Most reptiles catch live animals. To do this, they need to have good eyesight and be able to move quickly. Tortoises and iguanas eat plants and fruit.

▲ A chameleon shoots out its long, sticky tongue to catch insects.

Very large snakes kill prey by coiling their bodies around it and squeezing. They swallow the prey whole. These snakes are called constrictors.

▼ A snake can dislocate its lower jaw at the back of its mouth to swallow large prey. This rock python is swallowing a deer, which is much larger than its mouth.

Many snakes and lizards use their tongue to "taste" the ground or air. They follow the scent left by their prey.

Some reptiles use their bodies to lure prey. The snapping turtle attracts fish by wagging its tongue, which looks like a worm. The copperhead snake wiggles its tail to attract frogs.

▲ A monitor lizard "tastes" the air for signs of food or danger.

▼ Komodo dragons are the world's largest lizards, measuring up to 10 ft. (3 m) long. They eat animals such as wild pigs and deer.

◀ Crocodiles and alligators do not have chewing teeth, so they swallow small prey whole. They catch large prey and pull it underwater so that it drowns. Or they take large bites of flesh.

Avoiding predators

- Turtles and tortoises have a hard shell to protect them from predators.
- Chameleons change the color of their bodies to match their surroundings.
- If a lizard is attacked, it can shed its tail, which keeps wriggling while it escapes.
- Some reptiles are poisonous, a few have sharp spines, and some pretend to be dead.

▼ This tree boa constrictor is well hidden among the leaves, ready to attack its prey.

Hot and Cold

Reptiles are cold-blooded. This means that their body temperature changes with the temperature of the air or water around them.

▼ The gopher tortoise rests in its burrow during the hottest part of the day.

◀ This crocodile is opening its mouth wide so that the sun's heat warms the blood vessels in its mouth. This helps to warm its body.

Reptiles often bathe in the sun to warm their bodies. They will move into the shade if they become too hot.

▼ This marine iguana is sunbathing before swimming in the sea. It feeds on seaweed.

Reptiles become slow or do not move at all in cold weather. Those living in countries that have cold winters will hibernate.

Hot and cold facts

🐢 Reptiles' bodies are covered in scales, which keep their bodies from drying out.

🐢 Snakes need hot air temperatures to help them digest their food.

🐢 Thousands of male garter snakes hibernate together for warmth.

▲ These male garter snakes have just come out of hibernation. They have slept underground through the long Canadian winter.

Some lizards can make their skin change to a darker color. This happens because animals with dark-colored skin warm up more quickly in the sun.

▲ The Indian gavial spends the cold winter nights at the bottom of the river, where the water is a little warmer.

▲ This chameleon has become dark colored. The sun's heat will quickly warm its body.

Getting Around

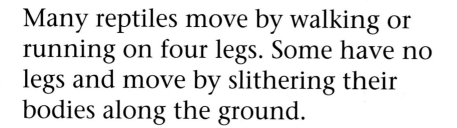

Many reptiles move by walking or running on four legs. Some have no legs and move by slithering their bodies along the ground.

▼ The gila monster is a slow-moving lizard. It lives in the rocky deserts of North America.

▲ The green turtle swims with the help of flippers. It can swim underwater for several hours without coming up for air.

Some reptiles are able to climb trees in search of food. Others spend most of their life in water.

The house gecko's special toe ▶ pads help it climb up walls and along ceilings.

Snakes grip the ground with large scales on their undersides. These scales help them to move along the ground or to climb trees.

When escaping from danger, some reptiles run on two legs. Sometimes this can be faster than running on four legs.

▲ The poisonous black mamba is the fastest snake. It can move up to 12 mph (19 km/h).

▼ The basilisk lizard can run for short distances on the surface of water. Basilisk lizards are sometimes called Jesus lizards.

Moving about

🐢 The giant tortoise moves very slowly. Its fastest speed is about 4 mph (6.4 km/h), which is the average person's walking speed.

🐢 The flying gecko has webbed feet and a skin flap that help it glide from tree to tree.

This boa constrictor ▶
is climbing a tree, using
its large scales to grip
the tree trunk.

19

Reptile Young

Some female reptiles lay eggs. They bury their eggs on land. Even sea turtles return to land to lay their eggs.

▼ Female Pacific green turtles come ashore to lay their eggs. They bury them on a sandy beach. Most then return to the sea.

Not all reptiles lay eggs. Many give birth to live young, which develop inside the female parent.

◀ A newborn baby boa constrictor, still in its egg sac

▼ A female tree python coils around her eggs to keep them warm. You can see one of the baby pythons just hatching.

▲ These ribbon snakes are courting. They coil around each other. Their "courtship dance" may last an hour.

Some reptiles perform a special "courtship dance" when they are ready to mate. This may mean a lot of movement, or a simple "head bobbing."

A male frilled lizard raises its ▶ neck frill and hisses to chase away another male.

Most reptiles do not look after their eggs or their young. They bury the eggs in the ground and leave the young to hatch.

Reptile eggs

- Reptile eggs have tough, leathery shells.
- Young snakes have a special egg tooth to cut their way out of the egg when they hatch.
- Baby crocodiles call to their mother when they are ready to hatch.

▼ A mother crocodile carefully looks after her newly hatched young. She carries them to the water in her mouth and will stay with them for a few weeks.

Pet Reptiles

Reptiles are not easy animals to keep as pets. Most need a great deal of care and special food.

◀ Geckos can be kept as pets. This leopard gecko needs to be handled very carefully. It may shed its tail if frightened.

Looking after reptiles

- Pet reptiles must be kept in a tank with air holes and a tight-fitting lid.
- Use a special "sunlight" bulb to light the tank.
- Use a heat lamp to keep the tank at the correct temperature.
- Put tree branches, bark, and rocks in the tank.
- Remember that some reptiles need to feed on live animals.

Many people are afraid of snakes, even though most are harmless. Keeping a snake as a pet can be rewarding. It can show people that if treated carefully, snakes are not frightening.

This child is handling a pet python. ▶

▼ Tortoises have always been popular pets. They usually need a warm, dark place in which to hibernate during the winter.

Unusual Reptiles

▲ Tuataras have lived on earth for millions of years, since before the time of the dinosaurs. They now live only in New Zealand.

Many species of reptiles have existed since the time of the dinosaurs, over 65 million years ago. Some have changed very little since. They have strangely shaped features.

Strange facts

- The Marion's tortoise is thought to be the world's longest-lived animal. It can live for 150 years.

- The slow worm is a type of lizard that has no legs. It is often mistaken for a snake.

▲ This poisonous sea snake lives in the sea, where it feeds on fish.

Reptiles adapted to live at a time when there were a lot of large predators. Most of them were also reptiles. Reptiles may have needed to protect themselves by looking very fierce.

A chameleon can turn its eyes so that one ▶ eye looks forward while the other looks behind.

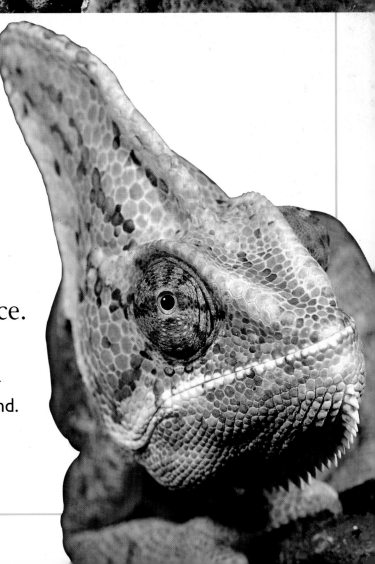

Scale of Reptiles

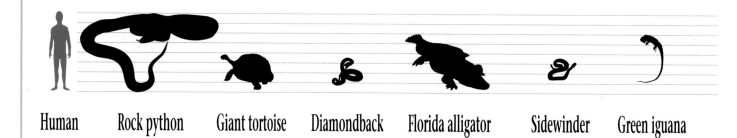

| Human | Rock python | Giant tortoise | Diamondback rattlesnake | Florida alligator | Sidewinder snake | Green iguana |

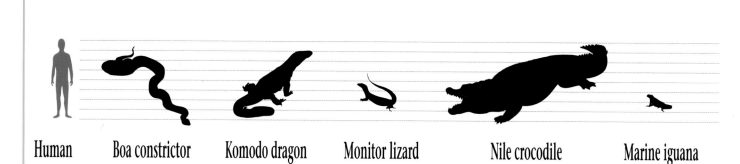

| Human | Boa constrictor | Komodo dragon | Monitor lizard | Nile crocodile | Marine iguana |

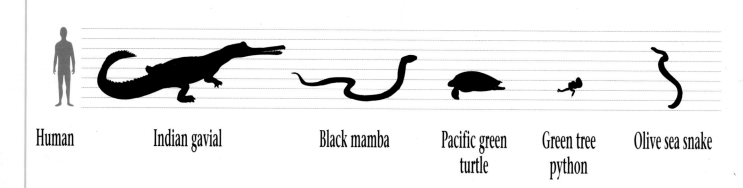

| Human | Indian gavial | Black mamba | Pacific green turtle | Green tree python | Olive sea snake |

Mediterranean chameleon	Snake-necked turtle	Red-sided garter snake	Gila monster	Human hand

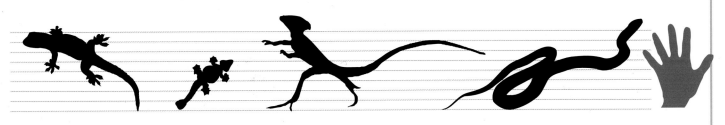

Tokay gecko	Flying gecko	Basilisk lizard	Ribbon snake	Human hand

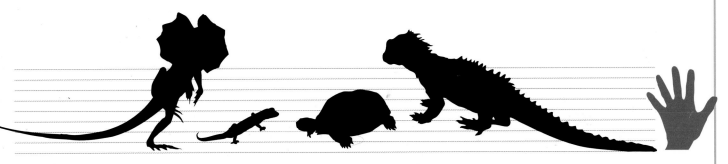

Frilled lizard	Leopard gecko	Hermann's tortoise	Tuatara	Human hand

Glossary

Antarctic The region at or around the South Pole.

Blood vessels Veins and arteries that carry blood around the body.

Burrow A hole dug in the ground by some animals for shelter.

Constrictors Very large snakes, including boa constrictors and pythons, which kill their prey by coiling their bodies around it and squeezing.

Courtship dance A dance performed to attract a mate.

Crocodilians Crocodiles, alligators, gavials, and caimans.

Dinosaurs Huge, four-footed reptiles that lived over 65 million years ago.

Dislocate To displace bones in the case of snakes to temporarily move the jawbones out of their joints.

Hibernate To spend the winter in an inactive state resembling sleep.

Predators Animals that hunt others for food.

Prey Animals that are hunted and killed for food.

Scales Thin bony or horny overlapping plates protecting the skin of reptiles and fish.

Books to Read

Burton, John A. *Reptile* (3-D Eyewitness). New York: Dorling Kindersley, 1998.

Dussling, Jennifer. *Slinky, Scaly Snakes*. New York: Dorling Kindersley, 1998.

Kalman, Bobbie. *What Is a Reptile?* (Science of Living Things). New York: Crabtree Publishing, 1999.

Miller-Schroeder, Pat. *Scales, Slime, and Salamanders: Reptiles and Amphibians* (Science at Work). Austin, TX: Raintree Steck-Vaughn, 2000.

Nature Encyclopedia. New York: Dorling Kindersley, 1998.

Silverstein, Alvin. *Snakes and Such* (What a Pet). Brookfield, CT: 21st Century Books, 1999.

Index

Page numbers in **bold** refer to photographs.

Picture acknowledgments

Bruce Coleman 17(t), /John Cancalosi cover (main picture), 5, /Rod Williams 7(t), /Joe McDonald 7(b), /Gunter Ziesler 9, /Fred Bruemmer 14, /MPL Fogden 15(t) and 17(b), /Allan Potts 20, /Alain Compost 22(b) and contents page, /Leonard Lee Rue 25(b), /Gerald Cubitt 26, /Joe McDonald 27(b); Frank Lane Picture Agency /Martin Withers 6, /Brake/Sunset 23; NHPA Anthony Bannister 10(t), /Philippa Scott 10(b), /Jany Sauvanet 11(b), /A.N.T. 13(t) and title page, /Martin Harvey 13(b), /Stephen Dalton 15(b) and title page inset, /Daniel Heuclin 16. /Anthony Bannister 18(t), Stephen Dalton 18(b), /Martin Harvey 19, /Daniel Heuclin 21(t), /Karl Switak 21(b), /Daniel Heuclin 24, /Joe Blossom 25(t); Oxford Scientic Films /Richard Packwood cover(inset), Mark Jones 4, /Stephen Downer 8-9, /David Dennis 12, /J. Gutierrez Acha 22(r), /Howard Hall 27(t); Wayland Picture Library/Julia Waterlow 11(t).